Contents

Introduction

If you are wild about learning and wild about animals – this book is for you!

It will take you on a wild adventure, where you will practise key grammar and punctuation skills and explore the amazing world of animals along the way.

Each grammar and punctuation topic is introduced in a clear and simple way with lots of interesting activities to complete so that you can practise what you have learned.

Alongside every grammar and punctuation topic you will uncover fascinating facts about the many different creatures who live in, on or by the world's seas and oceans. What is your favourite sea creature?

When you have completed each topic, record the animals that you have seen and the skills that you have learned in the explorer's logbook on pages 28–29.

Good luck, explorer!

Shelley Welsh

Capital letters

We use **capital letters** at the start of sentences, and for the names of people, places, days and months. We also use a capital letter when we write the word 'I'.

For example:

capital letter for person's name

My mum, **C**hloe and **I** went shopping to get new shoes.

capital letter at start of sentence

capital letter for word 'I'

capital letter for month of the year

On **T**uesday 8th **S**eptember we are going to **L**ondon.

capital letter for day of the week

capital letter for name of a place

Task 1 Decide why the underlined words in each sentence start with a capital letter. Put a tick in the correct column.

	Person's name	Place name	Day of the week	Month of the year
Last <u>Saturday</u>, I went to the aquarium in <u>Manchester</u>.				
Next <u>August</u>, we are going to <u>North America</u>.				
<u>Jack</u> saw a film about crabs in <u>London</u>.				

Task 2 What is wrong with each word in **red** in these sentences? Write the word correctly on the line.

a Erin and **i** hope that we will see horseshoe crabs when we go on holiday in **july**.

_____   _____

b We are going to the world's largest aquarium in **atlanta**, which is a city in **america**.

_____   _____

The horseshoe crab uses its tail to steer itself through the water or to flip itself over if it gets stuck upside down.

Task 3 Circle the words in the passage below that should start with a capital letter. The first one has been done for you. Write the correct version on the lines below.

(last) friday, rosewood primary went to blue planet aquarium in chester. we saw all sorts of underwater creatures. mrs smith said that we would be starting a project on sea life. my friend marcus and i took lots of photographs, which his dad, mr jones, is going to print out.

Last _____

_____

_____

_____

Now use your tail to steer to pages 28–29 to record what you have learned in your explorer's logbook.

Statements and questions

A sentence must start with a **capital letter** and end with a **full stop**, a **question mark** or an **exclamation mark**. There are different types of sentence.

A **statement** is a sentence that tells you something. It starts with a capital letter and ends with a full stop.

A shark has hundreds of teeth.

A **question** is a sentence that asks something. It starts with a capital letter and ends with a question mark.

What do sharks eat?

Task 1 Rewrite each sentence, using the correct punctuation.

a a shark can grow to be as big as a bus

_____

_____

b do all sharks eat meat

_____

c sharks hunt in packs

_____

d have you seen my book about sharks

_____

_____

Task 2

Decide whether each sentence is a statement or a question. Put a tick in the correct column.

Sentence	Statement	Question
Are there any sharks in Great Britain?		
Sharks have rows and rows of teeth.		
Which species of shark is the biggest?		
Only some species of shark attack humans.		

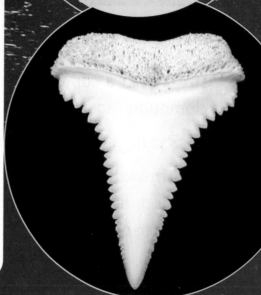

Task 3

What three questions would you ask a shark if it could speak?

Write your questions on the line. Remember to punctuate each one correctly.

a _____

_____

b _____

_____

c _____

_____

Now slice through the water to pages 28–29 to record what you have learned in your explorer's logbook.

Exclamations and commands

An **exclamation** is a sentence that shows a strong feeling, like anger, pain, delight or surprise. It starts with a capital letter and ends with an exclamation mark.

There's a huge shark following our boat!

A **command** is a sentence that tells you to do something. It starts with a capital letter and ends with either a full stop or an exclamation mark.

Look at that puffer fish.

The word *look* is a command verb. It is telling you what to do.

Task 1

Punctuate each sentence correctly. Write your sentence on the line.

a what an *enormous* puffer fish

_____

b look at that *amazing* coral

_____

c i can't believe how big that puffer fish can puff himself up

_____

_____

WILD FACT

One puffer fish has enough poison to kill 30 adults!

Task 2 Underline the command verb in each sentence.

a Watch the puffer fish carefully.

b Take a photograph of it swimming.

c Stick the photograph in your book.

d Write a sentence about it.

Task 3 Imagine that you are brave enough to tell a puffer fish what to do!

Write three commands that you would give it. An example has been done for you.

Show me how you puff yourself up. _____

a _____

b _____

c _____

Now puff yourself up and swim to pages 28–29 to record what you have learned in your explorer's logbook.

And, or and but

You can make one longer sentence from two shorter ones by joining words and clauses with **and**, **or** and **but**. The sentences must still make sense.

For example: *Ollie likes football. Ollie likes rugby.* These two sentences can be joined like this: *Ollie likes football and rugby.*

You can join: *Stella plays netball. She doesn't play tennis.*

Like this: *Stella plays netball but she doesn't play tennis.*

And: *Millie doesn't like peas. Millie doesn't like carrots.*

Can be written as: *Millie doesn't like peas or carrots.*

FACT FILE

Animal: Octopus
I live in: Shallow, warm tropical waters
I eat: Clams and crabs
I weigh: Up to 10 kg

Task 1

Write either **and** or **but** into these sentences so they make sense.

a I like oranges _____ apples.

b When I go swimming, I take my flippers _____ goggles.

c We can walk by the river _____ we have to be careful.

d Mum is taking me to the cinema _____ we are going to have popcorn.

e We like jam on our toast _____ we don't like butter.

Task 2   Insert **or**, **but** or **and** in the passage below.

Sea snails, squid, octopus, clams _____ oysters are all kinds of mollusc. They all look different _____ their bodies are similar. Molluscs have three body parts: a head, a soft bit inside the shell _____ a foot. They don't have eyes _____ ears _____ they can sense things.

WILD FACT

To escape from predators, an octopus squirts out a cloud of purple-black ink before swimming off.

Task 3   Underline the correct joining word in the brackets so that each sentence makes sense.

a   Octopuses live in either warm (**and** / **or** / **but**) cold waters.

b   Octopuses have a skull (**and** / **or** / **but**) no skeleton.

c   The arms of an octopus have suckers which allow it to grab (**and** / **or** / **but**) taste things.

d   You would think that an octopus's arms would get tangled up (**and** / **or** / **but**) they don't!

WILD FACT

An octopus can change the colour of its skin to match its surroundings and hide from animals that want to eat it!

Now squirt some ink and swim to pages 28–29 to record what you have learned in your explorer's logbook.

Joining clauses

We can use the words **when**, **if**, **that** and **because** to join two clauses, depending on what we are trying to say. For example:

*The photographers went out in the boat **because** they wanted to see some whales.*

*Our teacher told us to come inside **if** it started to rain.*

*We cheered the dancers **when** the performance was over.*

*The apples **that** we picked were green and red.*

Task 1   Use one of **when**, **if**, **that** or **because** to complete these sentences.

a The killer whales swam around that prey _____ they didn't want them to escape.

b The whale _____ wanted to talk to its friends whistled and clicked.

c I shouted out loud _____ I spotted the killer whale.

d We decided to take a video _____ we saw a killer whale.

Task 2 Underline the correct joining word in the brackets so that each sentence makes sense.

a Killer whales are easy to spot (**because** / **that**) they are black and white and have a large dorsal fin.

b The killer whales (**because** / **that**) we saw on our trip were huge.

c Sea creatures will suffer (**if** / **that**) we don't keep our oceans clean.

d Killer whales use high-pitched clicks (**that** / **when**) they talk to each other.

WILD FACT

Killer whales use echolocation (sound waves in the water) to find their prey.

WILD F

Killer whales talk to each other with screams, clicks and whistles or by slapping their flippers.

Task 3 Draw a line from each clause on the left to a clause on the right starting with **when**, **because** or **if** to make a sentence that makes sense.

a A killer whale uses echolocation

if they want to scare prey into the sea.

b Sea life is in danger

when it wants to catch its prey.

c Killer whales will sometimes slide on to a beach

because people put rubbish in the oceans.

Now slap your flippers to get to pages 28–29 to record what you have learned in your explorer's logbook.

11

Word classes

Nouns are naming words for objects, people and animals.

The girl walked her dog. The book is on the table.

Adjectives are describing words.

I am happy. The cat is furry.

Adverbs give more information about a verb. They often end in **ly**.

I wrote my name quickly.   She sang loudly.

Verbs are doing or being words.

*She drinks water every day.
Sam walked to school.*

FACT FILE

Animal:	Basking shark
I live in:	The sea, close to shores and just below the surface of the water
I eat:	A soup of tiny sea creatures called plankton
I weigh:	Up to 2,200 kg!

Task 1

Complete the table by writing each word in the correct column. Some examples have been done for you.

swiftly   shark   look
slowly   explorer   tightly
binoculars   dangerous   hold
vicious   catch   sharp

Word class			
Noun	**Adjective**	**Adverb**	**Verb**
mouth	huge	hungrily	eat

WILD FACT

Basking sharks might look fearsome, but they are completely harmless.

Task 2 Decide whether each word in bold in the sentences is an **adjective**, an **adverb**, a **verb** or a **noun**, then write your answer on the line.

a The shark **quickly** dived to the sea bed.

_____

b Basking sharks **swim** close to the water's surface.

_____

c **Tiny** plankton are the basking shark's main food.

_____

d Basking sharks like to stay close to the **shore**.

_____

WILD FACT

Basking sharks have huge mouths – they can be almost 1m wide!

Task 3 Hunt for these nouns, adjectives, adverbs and verbs in the word search. The first letter is in red to help you.

blue

dangerous

breathe

eat

explorer

cautiously

y	c	l	e	v	e	r	l	y	f
q	u	s	a	e	x	y	q	a	i
j	e	s	t	h	p	l	a	e	s
a	r	i	u	i	l	t	g	n	h
f	l	e	s	l	o	w	l	y	a
d	a	n	g	e	r	o	u	s	p
i	u	u	h	i	e	u	l	b	p
n	i	f	x	t	r	y	a	t	i
r	b	r	e	a	t	h	e	p	l
c	a	u	t	i	o	u	s	l	y

cleverly

happily

slowly

fin

fish

sea

Now sweep your way through the water to pages 28–29 to record what you have learned in your explorer's logbook.

13

Verbs – present tense

The **tense** of a verb tells us when we do things. When we are talking about something that is happening *now*, we use the **present tense**. There are two ways of writing the present tense.

I **read** my book every day. (= something I often do)

I **am reading** about the box jellyfish. (= something I am doing now)

FACT FILE

Animal: Box jellyfish
I live in: Coastal waters off Australia
I eat: Fish and shrimp
I weigh: Up to 2 kg

WILD FACT

The box jellyfish gets its name from the cube-like shape of its body.

| Task 1 | Circle the correct verb form in each sentence. |

a At the moment, I (**play** / **am playing**) tennis.

b My friend (**likes** / **is liking**) chocolate.

c Our parents (**enjoy** / **are enjoying**) their holiday.

d I (**brush** / **am brushing**) my teeth every morning.

Task 2 Choose the correct verb form from the choices in the brackets to complete each sentence.

WILD FACT

A box jellyfish's tentacles can reach up to 3 metres to stun or kill its prey.

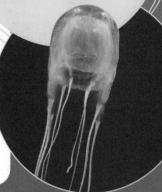

a A box jellyfish _____ quite fast. (**swim / is swimming / swims**)

b A box jellyfish _____ about 15 tentacles. (**is having / have / has**)

c A box jellyfish _____ its prey. (**is poisoning / poisons / poison**)

d The body of the box jellyfish _____ shaped like a cube. (**is being / are / is**)

Task 3 Solve the crossword, using the verb clues.

Across

1. I do this to my teeth and hair.

5. I do this with a ball.

6. I do this in the playground.

Down

2. I do this with my book.

3. I do this in my bed.

4. I do this in the sea.

5. I do this after I've made a mess!

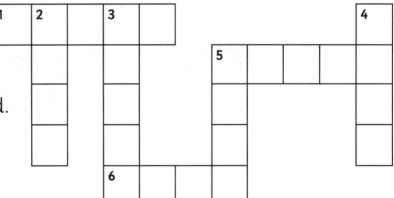

Now float to pages 28–29 to record what you have learned in your explorer's logbook.

Verbs – past tense

When we are talking about something that has already happened, we use the **past tense**. Here are two ways of writing the past tense.

*Yesterday, we **visited** the aquarium.*

*Yesterday, while we **were visiting** the aquarium, our teacher fell over.*

Task 1	Underline the correct form of the past tense in brackets in the following sentences.

a Yesterday, we (**visited** / **was visiting**) the aquarium.

b The sea otters (**was floating** / **were floating**) on the water.

c We (**saw** / **were seeing**) sea otters eating small shellfish and fish.

d The explorers (**were filming** / **has filmed**) a raft of sea otters.

WILD FACT

Sea otters float around together in groups called rafts. They wrap themselves in sea kelp (seaweed) so that they don't drift out to sea.

Task 2 Write these present tense sentences in the past tense.

a I am watching sea otters on the television.

_____

b I like the programme about sea otters very much!

_____

c There is a great book about sea creatures on the table.

_____

d We are writing about our aquarium trip.

_____

Task 3 Write 'present tense' or 'past tense' on the line for each of the verbs in bold in these sentences.

a Sea otters **are** carnivores.

_____

b We **saw** a sea otter floating on its back.

_____

c The sea otter **was eating** a fish.

_____

d Sea otters **smash** shellfish on rocks.

_____

e The sea otters **are looking** for food.

_____

Now swim to pages 28–29 to record what you have learned in your explorer's logbook.

Expanded noun phrases

When we want to give the reader more information about a noun, we use an **expanded noun phrase**. We can do this by adding an adjective to describe the noun. Remember, adjectives are describing words.

a cat → a **ginger** cat   the sky → the **cloudy** sky

the ginger cat and *the cloudy sky* are expanded noun phrases: *ginger* describes the cat and *cloudy* describes the sky.

WILD FACT

Hawksbill turtles are named after their narrow, pointed beak – it looks just like a hawk's beak!

Task 1 — Underline the expanded noun phrase in each sentence. Look for something that is being described. The first one has been done for you.

Turtles have <u>a bony shell</u>.

a The diver scratched his hand on the sharp coral reef.

b The transparent jellyfish swam away from a predator.

c We are studying interesting sea creatures at school.

Task 2 Choose adjectives to complete the passage below so that it contains expanded noun phrases.

hungry	white	frothy	female	sandy

We stood on the _____ beach to watch the _____ sea turtles laying eggs. There were _____, _____ waves, which may have been a sign of _____ predators.

WILD FACT

Although male turtles never leave the sea, females come ashore to lay eggs – to the same beach where they were hatched themselves!

Task 3 Make expanded noun phrases from each noun. Here are some adjectives to help you. The first one has been done for you.

salty	frothy	sharp	scaly	hard	silvery	puffy	scary

Noun	Expanded noun phrase
oyster	the silvery oyster
ocean	
killer whales	
puffer fish	

Now glide to pages 28–29 to record what you have learned in your explorer's logbook.

Commas in lists

When we are writing a list of things, we need a **comma** to separate each item. For example:

Mum and I bought apples, oranges, pears and bananas.

We do not put a comma before the word *and*.

WILD FACT

Steller sea lions can stay under water for up to 16 minutes without taking a breath!

FACT FILE

Animal: Steller sea lion
I live in: The Pacific Ocean
I eat: Squid, octopus and fish
I weigh: Up to 1,120 kg

Task 1

Insert the missing commas in the following sentences.

a The explorers put their notebooks pens binoculars and magnifying glasses into their backpacks.

b Our teacher gave us rulers pencils sharpeners and rubbers for the test.

c We bought cheese bread butter and milk from the shop.

d There were swings roundabouts slides and a see-saw in the park.

Task 2 Insert the missing commas in this short passage about sea lions.

We went to look at the Steller sea lions. They have ear flaps long fore-flippers and short hair. We saw bulls cows and pups on some rocks. They were eating squid octopus and fish. It was a long ride back to our hotel. We had to take a helicopter a train a bus and a taxi.

WILD FACT

A male sea lion is called a bull, a female is a cow and a baby is a pup.

Task 3 Write a list of at least three things you would want for each of these events.

Where you would go	Items you would take
On an adventure	I would take
The park on a snowy day	I would take
On holiday	I would take
A birthday party	I would take

Now wobble your way to pages 28–29 to record what you have learned in your explorer's logbook.

Apostrophes

Sometimes we make words shorter by taking away a letter or letters. We use an **apostrophe** to show where the missing letters would be. For example:

We are getting cold out here. → *We're getting cold out here.*

We're is the shortened form of *we are*. The missing letter is **a**. It is very important to put the apostrophe in the correct place – exactly above where the missing letters should be.

FACT FILE

Animal: Beluga whale
I live in: The Arctic Ocean
I eat: Fish, shellfish and worms
I weigh: 1,350 kg

Task 1 Match the words on the top row to their shortened form on the bottom row. One has been done for you.

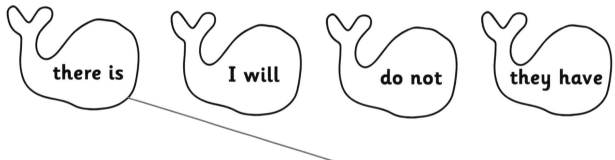

there is — I will — do not — they have

they've — don't — I'll — there's

Task 2 Rewrite the words on the left as one shorter word, using an apostrophe.

a I have ⟶ ☐

b she is ⟶ ☐

c they had ⟶ ☐

d you are ⟶ ☐

Task 3 Rewrite each sentence on the lines below, turning the words shown in **bold** into one word, using an apostrophe.

a **We have** been learning about beluga whales in class.

_____

b **There is** a nature programme about whales on TV tonight.

_____

c **I am** going to watch it with my dad.

_____

d **He has** already said that I can stay up late!

_____

Now swim backwards to pages 28–29 to record what you have learned in your explorer's logbook.

23

Apostrophes to show belonging

When we want to show that something belongs to someone, we can use an **apostrophe**. For example:

My sister's coat is on the peg.
(the coat belongs to my sister)

Sam has lost his dog's collar.
(the collar belongs to the dog)

It is very important that you put the apostrophe in the correct place, between the last letter of the word and the letter 's'.

FACT FILE

Animal: Stingray
I live in: Coastal waters
I eat: Crabs, clams, oysters and sea snails
I weigh: Up to 350 kg

Task 1 Insert the missing apostrophe in the correct place in each sentence.

a The stingray s tail has a poisonous stinger.

b Our teacher s husband saw a stingray on holiday.

c He was going to take a photograph with his cousin s camera.

d Unfortunately, he had left it at his friend s house.

WILD FACT

To swim, a stingray flaps its fins like a bird and flies through the water!

Task 2

Change the phrases on the left so that they use an apostrophe to show that something belongs to someone. Write the new phrase on the line. The first one has been done for you.

a the pen belonging to my sister   <u>my sister's pen</u>

b the ball belonging to Liam   _____

c the bowl belonging to the dog   _____

d the rays belonging to the sun   _____

WILD FACT

Stingrays use a poisonous stinger on their tail to defend themselves.

Task 3

Add an apostrophe and the letter **s** to the words in the box and then complete the sentence.

stingray	class	Lucy	boat

a The _____ eyes are on the top of its head.

b Our _____ new topic is sea creatures.

c _____ picture of a stingray has been put on the wall.

d The _____ engine has broken.

Now fly under the water to pages 28–29 to record what you have learned in your explorer's logbook.

Quick test

Now try these questions. Give yourself 1 mark for every correct answer.

1 **Insert the missing apostrophes to show *belonging* in this sentence.**

My brothers teddy is on my sisters bed. ☐

2 **Change the present tense verbs in brackets into the past tense. Write the past tense verb on the line.**

a I (eat) _____ my breakfast at 8 o'clock. ☐

b My mum (makes) _____ me wipe my feet. ☐

3 **Write the words in *bold* as one word by using an apostrophe to replace missing letters.**

I (**could not**) _____ believe that they (**did not**) _____ win the match after (**they had**) _____ practised so hard. ☐

4 **Insert either *and*, *or*, or *but* in these sentences.**

I enjoy English _____ not maths. I like both art _____ PE. We can choose a story _____ a film on the last day of term. ☐

5 **Write these sentences correctly, remembering to use the correct punctuation.**

a look at the electric eels _____ ☐

b there are so many _____ ☐

c have you seen the sharks _____ ☐

6 **Tick the box to show whether each word is an adjective, a noun, a verb or an adverb.** ☐

Word	Adjective	Noun	Verb	Adverb
eat				
swiftly				
fin				
shiny				

7 **Insert the missing commas in this sentence.**
I am going to take a notebook a waterproof coat a camera and some binoculars on my whale-watching trip.

8 **Underline the *two* expanded noun phrases in this sentence.**

We all thought that the poisonous stingray was the best creature.

9 **Rewrite this sentence using correct punctuation.**

my brother and i went to scotland in the summer

_____

_____

10 **Use *when*, *if*, *that* or *because* to join these clauses.**

a I go to bed _____ I've brushed my teeth.

b I have porridge for breakfast _____ it is healthy.

c I have toast _____ I have time.

d I take the packed lunch _____ mum has made.

11 **Change these verbs from the past tense into the present tense.**

swam _____   attacked _____

12 **Underline the word in this sentence that tells you it is a command.**

Finish your homework quickly.

13 **Write the verbs in these sentences then change them from the present tense to the past tense.**

a I am reading my book.

Verb: _____   Past tense: _____

b Milo and Jack are jumping into the pool.

Verb: _____   Past tense: _____

How did you do?   1–5 Try again!   6–10 Good try!
11–15 Great work!   16–20 Excellent exploring!

/20

27

Explorer's Logbook

Tick off the topics as you complete them and then colour in the star.

How do you feel?
- Needs practice
- Nearly there
- Got it!

Capital letters ☐

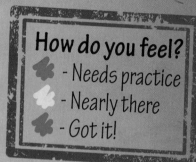

Statements and questions ☐

Exclamations and commands ☐

And, or and but ☐

Joining clauses ☐

Word classes ☐

Verbs – present tense ☐

Verbs – past tense ☐

Expanded noun phrases ☐

Commas in lists ☐

Apostrophes ☐

Apostrophes to
show belonging ☐

Answers

Pages 2–3
Task 1

	Person's name	Place name	Day of the week	Month of the year
Last <u>Saturday</u>, I went to the aquarium in <u>Manchester</u>.		✓	✓	
Next <u>August</u>, we are going to <u>North America</u>.		✓		✓
<u>Jack</u> saw a film about crabs in <u>London</u>.	✓	✓		

Task 2
a I, July
b Atlanta, America

Task 3
Last **F**riday, **R**osewood **P**rimary went to **B**lue **P**lanet **A**quarium in **C**hester. **W**e saw all sorts of underwater creatures. **M**rs **S**mith said that we would be starting a project on sea life. **M**y friend **M**arcus and **I** took lots of photographs, which his dad, **M**r **J**ones, is going to print out.

Pages 4–5
Task 1
a A shark can grow to be as big as a bus.
b Do all sharks eat meat?
c Sharks hunt in packs.
d Have you seen my book about sharks?

Task 2

Are there any sharks in Great Britain?	Question
Sharks have rows and rows of teeth.	Statement
Which species of shark is the biggest?	Question
Only some species of shark attack humans.	Statement

Task 3
Answers will vary. Each question to start with a capital letter and end with a question mark.

Pages 6–7
Task 1
a **W**hat an enormous puffer fish!
b **L**ook at that amazing coral!
c **I** can't believe how big that puffer fish can puff himself up!

Task 2
a <u>Watch</u> the puffer fish carefully.
b <u>Take</u> a photograph of it swimming.
c <u>Stick</u> the photograph in your book.
d <u>Write</u> a sentence about it.

Task 3
Answers will vary. Each sentence should contain a command verb and end with a full stop or an exclamation mark, e.g. *Eat those worms. Swim this way. Follow that shark.*

Pages 8–9
Task 1
a I like oranges **and** apples.
b When I go swimming, I take my flippers **and** goggles.
c We can walk by the river **but** we have to be careful.
d Mum is taking me to the cinema **and** we are going to have popcorn.
e We like jam on our toast **but** we don't like butter.

Task 2
Sea snails, squid, octopus, clams **and** oysters are all kinds of mollusc. They all look different **but** their bodies are similar. Molluscs have three body parts: a head, a soft bit inside the shell **and** a foot. They don't have eyes **or** ears **but** they can sense things.

Task 3
a or   b but   c and   d but

Pages 10–11
Task 1
a The killer whales swam around their prey **because** they didn't want them to escape.
b The whale **that** wanted to talk to its friends whistled and clicked.
c I shouted out loud **when** I spotted the killer whale.
d We decided to take a video **when** (or **if**) we saw a killer whale.

Task 2
a Killer whales are easy to spot **<u>because</u>** they are black and white and have a large dorsal fin.
b The killer whales **<u>that</u>** we saw on our trip were huge.
c Sea creatures will suffer **<u>if</u>** we don't keep our oceans clean.
d Killer whales use high-pitched clicks **<u>when</u>** they talk to each other.

Task 3
a A killer whale uses echolocation – when it wants to catch its prey.
b Sea life is in danger – because people put rubbish in the oceans.
c Killer whales will sometimes slide on to a beach – if they want to scare prey into the sea.

Pages 12–13
Task 1

Word class			
Noun	**Adjective**	**Adverb**	**Verb**
mouth	huge	hungrily	eat
shark	sharp	swiftly	catch
binoculars	vicious	slowly	hold
explorer	dangerous	tightly	look

Task 2
a quickly – adverb   b swim – verb
c tiny – adjective   d shore – noun

Task 3

```
y c l e v e r l y f
q u s a e x y q a i
j e s t h p l a e s
a r i u i l t g n h
f l e s l o w l y a
d a n g e r o u s p
i u u h i e u l b p
n i f x t r y a t i
r b r e a t h e p l
c a u t i o u s l y
```

Pages 14–15
Task 1
a At the moment, I **am playing** tennis.

b My friend **likes** chocolate.

c Our parents **are enjoying** their holiday.

d I **brush** my teeth every morning.

Task 2
a The box jellyfish **swims** / **is swimming** quite fast.

b The box jellyfish **has** about 15 tentacles.

c The box jellyfish **poisons** / **is poisoning** its prey.

d The body of the box jellyfish **is** shaped like a cube.

Task 3
Across

1 brush 5 throw 6 play

Down

2 read 3 sleep 4 swim 5 tidy

Pages 16–17
Task 1
a Yesterday, we **visited** the aquarium.

b The sea otters **were floating** on the water.

c We **saw** sea otters eating small shellfish and fish.

d The explorers **were investigating** a raft of sea otters.

Task 2
a I <u>was watching</u> sea otters on the television.

b I <u>liked</u> the programme about sea otters very much!

c There <u>was</u> a great book about sea creatures on the table.

d We <u>were</u> writing about our aquarium trip.

Task 3
a are – present tense b saw – past tense

c was eating – past tense d smash – present tense

e are looking – present tense

Pages 18–19
Task 1
a The diver scratched his hand on <u>the sharp coral reef</u>.

b <u>The transparent jellyfish</u> swam away from a predator.

c We are studying <u>interesting sea creatures</u> at school.

Task 2
We stood on the **sandy** beach to watch the **female** sea turtles laying eggs. There were **white**, **frothy** waves, which may have been a sign of **hungry** predators.

Task 3
Answers will vary. Examples:

the salty ocean

the scary killer whales

a puffy puffer fish

Pages 20–21
Task 1
a The explorers put their notebooks, pens, binoculars and magnifying glasses into their backpacks.

b Our teacher gave us rulers, pencils, sharpeners and rubbers for the test.

c We bought cheese, bread, butter and milk from the shop.

d There were swings, roundabouts, slides and a see-saw in the park.

Task 2
We went to look at the Steller sea lions. They have ear flaps, long fore-flippers and short hair. We saw bulls, cows and pups on some rocks. They were eating squid, octopus and fish. It was a long ride back to our hotel. We had to take a helicopter, a train, a bus and a taxi.

Task 3
Answers will vary. Lists of items must be separated by commas.

Pages 22–23
Task 1
there is – there's; I will – I'll; do not – don't; they have – they've

Task 2
a I have – I've b she is – she's

c they had – they'd d you are – you're

Task 3
a <u>We've</u> been learning about beluga whales in class.

b <u>There's</u> a nature programme about whales on TV tonight.

c <u>I'm</u> going to watch it with my dad.

d <u>He's</u> already said that I can stay up late!

Pages 24–25
Task 1
a The **stingray's** tail has a poisonous stinger.

b Our **teacher's** husband saw a stingray on holiday.

c He was going to take a photograph with his **cousin's** camera.

d Unfortunately, he had left it at his **friend's** house.

Task 2
a my sister's pen c the dog's bowl

b Liam's ball d the sun's rays

Task 3
a The stingray's eyes are on the top of its head.

b Our class's new topic is sea creatures.

c Lucy's picture of a stingray has been put on the wall.

d The boat's engine has broken.

Pages 26–27
1 My brother's teddy is on my sister's bed.

2 a ate b made

3 I **couldn't** believe that they **didn't** win the match after **they'd** practised so hard.

4 I enjoy English **but** not maths. I like both art **and** PE. We can choose a story **or** a film on the last day of term.

5 a Look at the electric eels. (or !)

b There are so many.

c Have you seen the sharks?

6 eat – verb; fin – noun; swiftly – adverb; shiny – adjective

7 I am going to take a notebook, a waterproof coat, a camera and some binoculars on my whale-watching trip.

8 We all thought that <u>the poisonous stingray</u> was <u>the best creature</u>.

9 My brother and I went to Scotland in the summer.

10 a I go to bed **when** I've brushed my teeth.

b I have porridge for breakfast **because** it is healthy.

c I have toast **if** (or **when**) I have time.

d I take the packed lunch **that** mum has made.

11 swam – swim; attacked – attack.

12 <u>Finish</u> your homework quickly.

13 a am reading / was reading

b are jumping / were jumping

Well done, explorer!

You have finished your grammar and punctuation adventure!

Explorer's pass

Name: _____

Age: _____

Date: _____

Draw a picture of yourself in the box!